Your Strategy, Your Success

The Essentials of Strategic Planning for Organizations

This book is dedicated to my father William (Bill) Chesnutt. My father passed away on February 17, 2023, after a yearlong battle with cancer. My dad spent his life in the oil and gas industry in positions from company owner to consultant. My dad spent his life as a rancher, musician, hard worker, and a family man. He enjoyed watching his horses' race competitively. Bill especially loved spending time writing music, singing, playing his guitar, and being with his friends and family.

The things I remember most about my father are the great times we had hunting, fishing, and camping when I was younger. I also think about the years he coached the baseball team I was on from t-ball through minor leagues. Those were some of the greatest times of my childhood.

He was one of the earliest sparks of my entrepreneurial spirit. I used to go to work with him when I was younger and he would always plan everything out on a piece of paper or napkin, pretty much anything that was around he could write on. He taught me to dream big and chase after those dreams.

I miss my father very much and will always be grateful for the time we had together.

Acknowledgements

In my first book I thanked many individuals that have had a great impact on my life. This time around I want to thank the organizations that are on the front lines every day helping people. This list will only contain those organizations that I have directly worked with or utilized services from.

Vets2Industry is a 501c3 organization with a mission of establishing connections, sharing knowledge, and identifying opportunities for veterans and their families. Their vision is to become the most comprehensive online information library of free resources, benefits, and services for the military community, their spouses, and their families. Brian Arrington is the Founder and continues to dedicate his life to helping veterans post his own personal service. Brian, thank you for all that you do to help the veteran community.

The Defeating Epilepsy Foundation is a 501c3 organization with a mission and vision to provide the advocacy and educational resources needed for the epilepsy community and our society. They are dedicated to removing the stigma associated with epilepsy and helping to create opportunities for individuals battling epilepsy. Natalie Boehm is the Founder and continues to dedicate her life to helping those effected by epilepsy through awareness and education. Natalie, thank you for your dedication to such a worthy cause.

Introduction

First off, congratulations on your purchase of this book! In today's rapidly changing business landscape, organizations face unprecedented challenges and uncertainties. Innovative technologies emerge, consumer preferences shift, and global markets evolve at an astonishing pace. In such an environment, strategic planning becomes not only valuable but essential for an organization's long-term success.

Strategic planning is the process of defining an organization's direction and formulating a roadmap to achieve its goals. It goes beyond day-to-day operations and focuses on positioning the organization for sustainable growth, competitive advantage, and adaptability to changing circumstances. By taking a proactive and systematic approach to strategy, organizations can navigate complexity, seize opportunities, and mitigate risks effectively.

When organizations engage in strategic planning, they gain a holistic understanding of their internal strengths, weaknesses, external opportunities, and threats. This process enables them to align their resources, capabilities, and aspirations with the ever-evolving demands of the market. By establishing a clear vision and mission, setting strategic objectives, and developing well-defined strategies, organizations can chart a course towards their desired future state.

The purpose of this book, "Your Strategy, Your Success," is to provide readers with a comprehensive and practical guide to strategic planning. It offers insights, strategies, and tools to help individuals and organizations develop a strategic mindset and effectively navigate the complexities of strategy formulation and execution.

The book is structured to guide readers through the strategic planning process, from understanding the fundamentals of strategy to implementing and sustaining a successful strategy. Each chapter explores key concepts, provides real-world examples, and offers actionable tips to enhance strategic thinking and decision-making.

Before delving into the strategic planning process, it is crucial to establish a clear understanding of what strategy truly means. Strategy encompasses more than setting goals or implementing tactics. It involves making deliberate choices about how an organization will allocate its resources and capabilities to create a unique and sustainable position in the marketplace. By understanding the nuances of strategy, readers will be better equipped to craft effective plans for success.

The strategic planning process serves as a roadmap for organizations to identify opportunities, set objectives, and execute strategies that align with their vision and mission. This chapter introduces the six essential steps of the strategic planning process:

Step 1: Assessing the Current Situation

This step involves conducting a thorough analysis of the internal and external factors that impact the organization. By assessing strengths, weaknesses, opportunities, and threats (swot analysis), organizations gain insights into their current position and the landscape in which they operate.

Step 2: Defining the Vision and Mission

A compelling vision serves as a guiding star, providing a clear picture of the desired future state. The mission statement articulates the organization's purpose, values, and core beliefs. Defining a powerful vision and mission sets the foundation for effective strategic planning.

Step 3: Setting Strategic Objectives

Strategic objectives are specific, measurable goals that drive the organization forward. By setting objectives that are aligned with the vision and mission, organizations create a clear path towards their desired outcomes.

Step 4: Developing Strategies

In this step, organizations generate strategic options and evaluate their viability based on internal capabilities, market conditions, and competitive factors. The selected strategies should leverage strengths, exploit opportunities, and mitigate weaknesses and threats.

Step 5: Implementing the Strategy

Implementation is where the strategic plan comes to life. By creating an actionable plan, allocating resources effectively, and assigning responsibilities, organizations increase the likelihood of successful strategy execution.

Step 6: Monitoring and Adapting

Monitoring the progress of the strategic plan is vital to ensure that objectives are being met and adjustments can be made when necessary. By establishing performance metrics, tracking milestones, and embracing a culture of continuous improvement, organizations can adapt to changing circumstances and stay on course.

Conclusion

The introduction chapter establishes the criticality of strategic planning and highlights the purpose and structure of the book. It underscores the importance of understanding strategy and provides a glimpse into the strategic planning process that will be explored in detail throughout the subsequent chapters. By embarking on this journey of strategic planning, you will gain the knowledge and tools to shape your own success and drive their organizations towards a prosperous future.

Chapter One: Understanding Strategy

Before delving into the strategic planning process, it is crucial to establish a clear understanding of what strategy truly means. Strategy encompasses more than setting goals or implementing tactics. It involves making deliberate choices about how an organization will allocate its resources and capabilities to create a unique and sustainable position in the marketplace. By understanding the nuances of strategy, readers will be better equipped to craft effective plans for success.

Defining Strategy

At its core, strategy is about making choices. It involves making decisions about what an organization will do and, more importantly, what it will not do. Strategy provides a framework for allocating resources and directing efforts towards achieving specific objectives. It guides decision-making at all levels of the organization and provides a sense of purpose and direction.

Strategic Thinking

Strategic thinking is a mindset that encourages individuals and organizations to approach challenges and opportunities from a strategic perspective. It involves looking beyond immediate concerns and considering the broader context and long-term implications of actions. Strategic thinkers ask probing questions, challenge assumptions, and consider alternative paths to achieve their goals.

Elements of effective strategy

Effective strategies share certain key elements that contribute to their success:

- Clear and compelling vision: a vision provides a compelling picture of the desired future state of the organization. It serves as a unifying force and motivates individuals to work towards a common goal.
- Analysis and understanding: strategy development requires a deep understanding of the internal and external factors that influence the organization. This includes assessing strengths, weaknesses, opportunities, and threats (swot analysis), analyzing market trends, and understanding the competitive landscape.
- Alignment with mission and values: a strategy should be aligned with the organization's mission and core values. It ensures that actions and decisions are consistent with the overall purpose and principles of the organization.
- Differentiation and competitive advantage: a successful strategy leverages the organization's unique capabilities and seeks to create a competitive advantage in the marketplace. This may involve offering differentiated products or services, targeting specific customer segments, or adopting innovative approaches.
- Flexibility and adaptability: strategy should be flexible enough to accommodate changing circumstances and adapt to new opportunities or challenges. It requires ongoing monitoring and adjustment to ensure its relevance and effectiveness.
- Implementation and execution: a well-defined strategy

must be effectively implemented and executed. This involves translating strategic plans into actionable steps, allocating resources, and establishing clear responsibilities and timelines.

Strategy vs. Goals and Tactics

Strategy should not be confused with goals or tactics. While goals are specific targets that an organization aims to achieve, strategy provides the overarching approach and direction for reaching those goals. Tactics, on the other hand, are the specific actions and methods employed to execute the strategy and achieve the goals. Strategy sets the framework, while goals and tactics are the building blocks for its implementation.

By developing a deep understanding of strategy, readers will be better equipped to approach the strategic planning process with clarity and purpose. They will gain the ability to think strategically, make informed decisions, and create a roadmap that leads to long-term success. In the subsequent chapters, we will delve into the practical aspects of the strategic planning process, empowering readers to develop and execute effective strategies tailored to their unique organizational needs.

Chapter Two: The Strategic Planning Process

THE STRATEGIC PLANNING process serves as a roadmap for organizations to identify opportunities, set objectives, and execute strategies that align with their vision and mission. This chapter introduces the six essential steps of the strategic planning process:

Step 1: Assessing the Current Situation

The first step in the strategic planning process involves conducting a comprehensive analysis of the organization's internal and external environment. This includes assessing the organization's strengths, weaknesses, opportunities, and threats (SWOT analysis). It also involves analyzing market trends, understanding customer needs, and evaluating the competitive landscape. By gaining a deep understanding of the current situation, organizations can identify areas for improvement and uncover potential avenues for growth.

Step 2: Defining the Vision and Mission

A clear and compelling vision sets the direction and inspires everyone within the organization. It articulates the desired future state and the organization's aspirations. The mission statement defines the organization's purpose, core values, and the value it seeks to create for its stakeholders. Defining a powerful vision and mission creates a shared sense of purpose, aligns efforts, and provides a foundation for strategic decision-making.

Step 3: Setting Strategic Objectives

Strategic objectives are specific, measurable goals that guide the organization's actions and progress towards its vision. These objectives are derived from the organization's vision and mission and provide a clear path for achieving them. Strategic objectives should be challenging yet attainable, and they should be aligned with the organization's values and long-term aspirations. By setting clear objectives, organizations provide a focus for decision-making and resource allocation.

Step 4: Developing Strategies

In this step, organizations generate strategic options and evaluate their viability based on the analysis of the current situation and the defined objectives. Strategies are how organizations achieve their objectives and realize their vision. They involve making choices about how to allocate resources, create differentiation, and respond to market dynamics. Strategies can encompass areas such as market positioning, product development, partnerships, or operational efficiencies. It is essential to consider various strategic options and select the ones that align best with the organization's capabilities and objectives.

Step 5: Implementing the Strategy

Implementation is where the strategic plan comes to life. It involves translating the selected strategies into action by developing a detailed action plan. The action plan outlines the specific steps, tasks, and timelines required to execute the strategy successfully. It also involves allocating resources effectively, communicating the strategy to stakeholders, and assigning responsibilities. Implementation requires effective coordination, communication, and monitoring to ensure that progress is made towards strategic objectives.

Step 6: Monitoring and Adapting

Monitoring the progress of the strategic plan is critical to ensure that objectives are being met and adjustments can be made when necessary. Organizations establish key performance indicators (KPIs) and metrics to track progress and evaluate the effectiveness of the strategy. Regular reviews and evaluations help identify areas of improvement, challenges, and emerging opportunities. This continuous monitoring and adaptation process allows organizations to respond to changes in the internal and external environment and make informed decisions to keep the strategy on track.

By following the strategic planning process, organizations can align their actions, resources, and capabilities with their vision and mission. It provides a structured approach to strategic decision-making, increases organizational focus, and enhances the chances of achieving long-term success. In the subsequent chapters, we will delve deeper into each step of the process, providing practical tools and guidance to navigate the complexities of strategic planning and execution.

Chapter Three: Essential Components of Successful Strategy

A SUCCESSFUL STRATEGY is the backbone of organizational success. It provides a roadmap for achieving objectives, guiding decision-making, and positioning the organization for long-term growth. This chapter explores the essential components that contribute to the effectiveness of a strategy.

Clear and Compelling Vision

A clear and compelling vision provides a shared understanding of the desired future state of the organization. It serves as a guiding star, inspiring and motivating individuals within the organization. A strong vision creates a sense of purpose and direction, aligns efforts, and acts as a beacon for decision-making.

Analysis and Understanding

A successful strategy is built upon a deep understanding of the internal and external factors that impact the organization. This involves conducting thorough analysis, such as swot (strengths, weaknesses, opportunities, and threats) analysis, market research, and competitive analysis. By understanding the organization's strengths, weaknesses, market trends, and competitive landscape, strategic planners can identify opportunities and address challenges effectively.

Alignment with Mission and Values

A strategy should be aligned with the organization's mission and core values. The mission statement reflects the organization's purpose, values, and principles. When a strategy is aligned with the mission and values, it ensures that all actions and decisions are consistent with the organization's overarching purpose and beliefs.

Differentiation and Competitive Advantage

Successful strategies seek to create a competitive advantage by leveraging the organization's unique strengths and capabilities. This involves identifying areas where the organization can differentiate itself from competitors, whether through superior products or services, innovative approaches, superior customer experience, or cost leadership. By creating a competitive advantage, organizations can position themselves uniquely in the marketplace, attract customers, and outperform competitors.

Flexibility and Adaptability

In a dynamic business environment, successful strategies must be flexible and adaptable. The ability to respond to changes in the internal and external environment is crucial for sustained success. Strategies should be designed to accommodate unforeseen challenges, capitalize on emerging opportunities, and adjust to evolving market conditions. This requires a culture of continuous learning, agility, and a willingness to make necessary adjustments when needed.

Implementation and Execution

A well-defined strategy is only effective if it can be successfully implemented and executed. This involves translating the strategic plan into actionable steps, allocating resources effectively, and establishing clear responsibilities and timelines. Effective implementation requires strong leadership, effective communication, stakeholder engagement, and robust project management practices. It is essential to monitor progress, track key performance indicators, and address any barriers or challenges that arise during execution.

Continuous Monitoring and Evaluation

Successful strategies require ongoing monitoring and evaluation to ensure their relevance and effectiveness. Regular review of performance metrics, milestones, and key indicators helps identify areas of improvement, measure progress, and make informed decisions. By monitoring the strategy's performance, organizations can detect deviations, learn from experiences, and adapt the strategy as needed to stay on course towards achieving objectives.

By incorporating these essential components into strategic planning, organizations can develop effective strategies that drive success and sustainable growth. Each component plays a crucial role in guiding decision-making, aligning efforts, and creating a competitive advantage. In the subsequent chapters, we will delve deeper into each component, providing practical insights and tools to enhance strategic planning and execution.

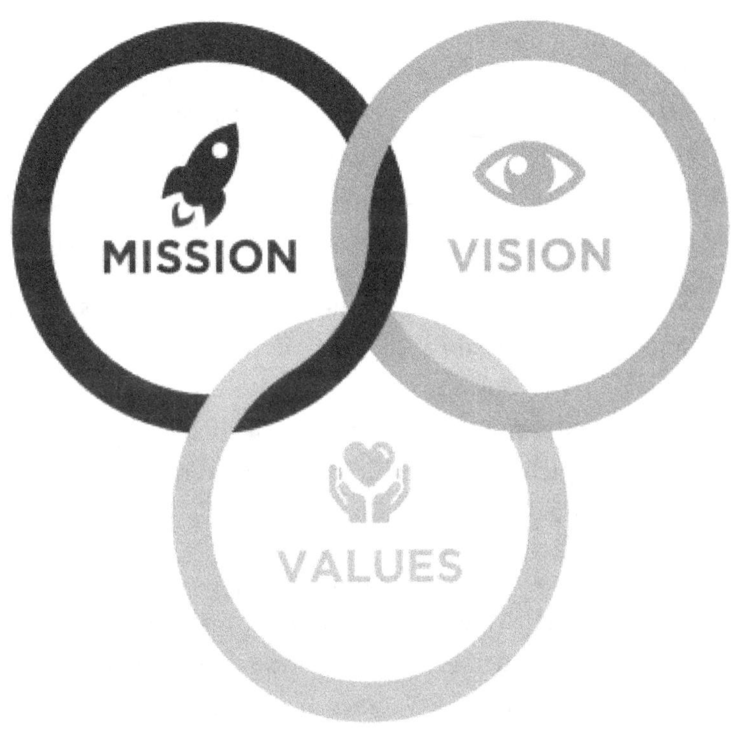

Chapter Four: Defining Your Mission, Vision, and Values

AS YOU CAN SEE FROM the previous chapters, the Mission, Vision, and Values of an organization are the foundation that all objectives and planning are based on. They define what you do, provide, who your customers are, where the organization sees itself in 20 years, and the guiding values that should be present in everything the organization does. Here's an explanation of each term:

Mission: The mission statement defines the core purpose of the organization. It describes what the organization does, who it serves, and the value it provides to its stakeholders. The mission statement outlines the reason for the organization's existence and acts as a compass for decision-making and strategic direction.

Vision: The vision statement outlines the desired future state or the long-term aspirations of the organization. It articulates the organization's ideal position or achievements it seeks to attain. A vision statement inspires and motivates stakeholders by painting a compelling picture of the future and guiding their efforts toward a common goal.

Values: Values represent the guiding principles and beliefs that shape the culture, behavior, and decision-making within the organization. They define the organization's ethical standards, expectations, and priorities. Values provide a framework for how employees interact, make decisions, and conduct themselves in alignment with the organization's mission and vision.

Mission

An organization's Mission statement should identify the organization's primary purpose and the needs it aims to fulfill, determine the target audience or stakeholders the organization serves, define the unique value or benefit the organization provides to its stakeholders, and create a concise, clear, and memorable statement that captures the essence of the organization's mission. Some of the key questions that a Mission statement should answer are:

- What is the core purpose of the organization?
- Who are the primary stakeholders or target audience?
- What value does the organization provide to its stakeholders?
- How does the organization differentiate itself from competitors?

The following is an example mission statement:

To empower businesses with innovative technology solutions, driving their growth and success in the digital age.

Vision

An organization's Vision statement explain what the organization envisions as its future state and/or long-term aspirations, consider the desired impact, growth, or achievements the organization seeks, make the vision statement inspirational, ambitious, and aligned with the organization's values and purpose, and craft a statement that paints a vivid and compelling picture of the organization's desired future. Some of the key questions that a Vision statement should answer are:

- What is the desired future state or long-term aspirations of the organization?
- What impact or achievements does the organization aim to accomplish?

- How does the vision inspire and motivate stakeholders?
- Is the vision aligned with the organization's mission and values?

The following is an example mission statement:

To be the leading provider of cutting-edge technology solutions, revolutionizing industries and transforming the way businesses operate globally.

Values

An organization's Values should reflect on the fundamental principles and beliefs that guide the organization's culture and behavior, identify the values that are important to the organization and reflect its identity and aspirations, determine the ethical standards, attitudes, and behaviors the organization expects from its employees, and create a concise set of values that represent the organization's core principles. Some of the key questions that a Values statement should answer are:

- What are the fundamental principles and beliefs that guide the organization's culture?
- What behaviors and attitudes are expected from employees?
- How do the values align with the organization's mission and vision?
- How are the values reinforced and integrated into the organization's practices and decision-making?

The following is an example of organizational values:

Innovation: We embrace continuous innovation, pushing boundaries, and challenging the status quo to deliver game-changing solutions.

Collaboration: We foster a culture of collaboration, working closely with clients, partners, and employees to achieve shared success.

Integrity: We conduct our business with the highest level of integrity, ethics, and transparency, earning the trust and respect of our stakeholders.

Customer-Centricity: We prioritize our customers' needs and deliver exceptional value, ensuring their satisfaction and long-term partnerships.

These statements provide a clear direction for the organization, guiding its strategic decisions, inspiring its employees, and communicating its identity and values to stakeholders.

A word of caution, when crafting any of these statements, do not write what you cannot or will not deliver. Writing something because it sounds good and not delivering can destroy the brand the organization is trying to build. Be honest and transparent in what you can provide and how you will do it. People and organizations will admire and trust the organization more when they represent themselves authentically.

Chapter Five: Allocating Resources

RESOURCE ALLOCATION, within the context of strategic planning, refers to the process of distributing and allocating the available resources of an organization effectively and efficiently to support the achievement of its strategic objectives. It involves making decisions about the allocation of financial resources, materials, and human resources in a manner that optimizes the organization's performance and maximizes the impact of its strategic initiatives.

Financial Resource Allocation

Financial resource allocation involves determining how financial resources, such as budget, capital, and investments, are allocated across various activities and projects to support the organization's strategic objectives. This includes considerations such as:

Budgeting: Allocating financial resources to different departments, projects, or initiatives based on their strategic importance and potential return on investment.

Capital Investment: Determining the allocation of funds for long-term investments in areas such as research and development, technology upgrades, infrastructure, or expansion into new markets.

Cost Management: Identifying cost-saving opportunities, optimizing expenses, and reallocating resources to areas that provide the highest value and align with strategic priorities.

Some examples of financial resource allocation are:

- Allocating a larger portion of the budget to research and development initiatives to drive innovation and develop new products or services aligned with the organization's strategic objectives.
- Investing in marketing and advertising campaigns to enhance brand awareness and market penetration in target markets identified in the strategic plan.
- Allocating funds for training programs and professional development to enhance the skills and knowledge of employees, aligning with strategic goals of building a high-performing workforce.

Material Resource Allocation

Material resource allocation involves the allocation of physical resources, such as raw materials, equipment, inventory, and facilities, to support the organization's strategic objectives. Considerations include:

Supply Chain Management: Ensuring a reliable and efficient supply chain that delivers the necessary materials and resources to support strategic initiatives.

Inventory Management: Optimizing inventory levels to avoid shortages or excess, aligning with demand forecasts and production requirements.

Asset Utilization: Maximizing the utilization of physical assets, such as machinery or facilities, to enhance productivity and operational efficiency.

Some examples of material resource allocation are:

- Prioritizing the procurement and allocation of raw materials and components required to produce key products or services identified as strategic priorities.
- Allocating manufacturing capacity and resources to product lines or segments that have higher growth potential and are aligned with the organization's strategic direction.
- Investing in upgraded technology and equipment to improve operational efficiency and support the organization's strategic goals of process optimization and cost reduction.

People Resource Allocation

People resource allocation involves strategically assigning and deploying human resources to areas that align with the organization's strategic objectives. It includes:

Workforce Planning: Assessing the skills, competencies, and capacity required to achieve strategic objectives and ensuring the organization has the right talent in the right roles.

Talent Development: Investing in training, development, and career progression opportunities to enhance the capabilities of employees and align their skills with strategic needs.

Team Allocation: Assigning individuals or teams to specific projects, initiatives, or departments based on their expertise, experience, and alignment with strategic priorities.

Some examples of people resource allocation are:

- Assigning skilled employees to cross-functional project teams focused on strategic initiatives, ensuring that key projects have the necessary expertise and resources to succeed.
- Developing a talent acquisition strategy to attract and recruit individuals with specific skills or experiences required to drive the organization's strategic objectives.
- Implementing a performance management system that aligns individual goals and objectives with the strategic priorities of the organization, ensuring that employees' efforts are directed toward the achievement of strategic goals.

These examples demonstrate how resource allocation decisions can directly support the implementation of strategic plans. By strategically allocating financial resources, materials, and human resources, organizations can ensure that they are investing in the areas that will have the greatest impact on achieving their strategic objectives and driving long-term success.

In strategic planning, effective resource allocation requires considering the organization's strategic goals, evaluating the potential risks and rewards of different allocation decisions, and aligning resources with the priorities that will drive the greatest value and impact. It involves a continuous evaluation and adjustment process to ensure that resources are deployed efficiently and effectively to support the organization's strategic initiatives and overall success.

Chapter Six: Overcoming Challenges and Pitfalls

WHILE STRATEGIC PLANNING offers tremendous benefits, it is not without its challenges and pitfalls. This chapter explores common obstacles that organizations may encounter during the strategic planning process and provides strategies for overcoming them.

Lack of Clarity and Alignment

One of the primary challenges in strategic planning is a lack of clarity and alignment among stakeholders. If there is confusion or disagreement about the organization's vision, mission, or strategic objectives, it can hinder progress. To overcome this challenge, it is crucial to foster open and transparent communication, engage stakeholders in the planning process, and ensure that everyone shares a collective understanding of the strategic direction. Regular feedback loops, workshops, and collaborative discussions can help align perspectives and foster a sense of ownership.

Insufficient Analysis and Understanding

Inadequate analysis of the internal and external environment is a significant pitfall that can undermine the strategic planning process and lead to flawed decision-making. To ensure the development of robust strategies, organizations must invest sufficient time, effort, and resources into conducting thorough analysis of various factors that influence their business landscape.

Comprehensive Research: Organizations need to engage in comprehensive research to gather relevant information. This includes studying industry trends, market dynamics, technological advancements, regulatory changes, and socio-cultural factors that impact their business. By staying informed about the latest developments, organizations can anticipate changes and proactively respond to them.

Data Gathering: Gathering accurate and reliable data is crucial for informed decision-making. Organizations should employ various methods to collect data, including surveys, interviews, market research, and analysis of internal data. Quantitative data provides valuable insights into customer preferences, market size, and financial performance, while qualitative data offers a deeper understanding of customer behaviors, emerging trends, and competitor strategies.

Analysis of Market Trends: Analyzing market trends helps organizations identify emerging opportunities and threats. It involves monitoring consumer preferences, technological advancements, economic indicators, and social shifts. By understanding these trends, organizations can adjust their strategies accordingly, identify niche markets, and stay ahead of competitors.

Understanding Customer Needs: Organizations must gain a deep understanding of their target customers and their evolving needs. This involves analyzing customer behavior, conducting surveys, and utilizing customer feedback mechanisms. By understanding customer pain points, preferences, and expectations, organizations can tailor their strategies to deliver superior value and enhance customer satisfaction.

Competitor Analysis: Analyzing competitors provides insights into their strategies, strengths, weaknesses, and positioning in the market. It helps organizations identify competitive advantages, potential threats, and areas for differentiation. By understanding competitor dynamics, organizations can develop strategies that capitalize on market gaps and outperform rivals.

SWOT Analysis: Conducting a thorough SWOT (Strengths, Weaknesses, Opportunities, Threats) analysis is a valuable tool for strategy formulation. It helps organizations identify their internal strengths and weaknesses while identifying external opportunities and threats. This analysis provides a holistic view of the organization's competitive position, highlighting areas that require improvement and uncovering strategic opportunities.

Scenario Planning: Organizations should engage in scenario planning to anticipate and prepare for various future scenarios. By considering alternative future outcomes and their potential impacts, organizations can develop strategies that are robust and flexible enough to withstand different market conditions. Scenario planning enables organizations to be proactive rather than reactive, reducing risks and enhancing their ability to capitalize on opportunities.

By investing in comprehensive analysis of the internal and external environment, organizations can make more informed and data-driven decisions. Thorough research and data gathering provide the necessary foundation for strategic planning, allowing organizations to mitigate risks, leverage strengths, capitalize on opportunities, and achieve their desired outcomes. Furthermore, continuous monitoring and reassessment of the environment ensures that strategies remain relevant and adaptable in the face of changing circumstances.

Lack of Flexibility and Adaptability

Strategies must be flexible and adaptable to navigate the ever-changing business landscape. Organizations that rigidly adhere to a fixed plan may miss emerging opportunities or fail to respond effectively to unforeseen challenges. It is important to build flexibility in the strategic planning process and foster a culture that embraces change. Regular monitoring, ongoing evaluation, and periodic strategy reviews enable organizations to make timely adjustments and pivot when needed.

Inadequate Implementation and Execution

A well-crafted strategy is meaningless without effective implementation and execution. Poor execution can undermine even the most brilliant strategy. To overcome this challenge, organizations should establish clear action plans, define responsibilities, allocate resources appropriately, and provide necessary support and training to teams. Effective project management practices, regular communication, and strong leadership are vital for successful execution.

Resistance to Change

Resistance to change is a common barrier in the strategic planning process. People are naturally inclined to stick to familiar routines and may resist new initiatives or ways of doing things. To overcome resistance, organizations must communicate the rationale behind the strategy, address concerns, and involve employees in the planning and decision-making process. Change management strategies, including education, training, and ongoing support, can help individuals embrace and adapt to new strategies.

To address resistance effectively, organizations must employ various strategies that foster understanding, engagement, and support among employees:

Communicating the Rationale: Clear and transparent communication is key to overcoming resistance. It is essential to communicate the rationale behind the strategy, including the reasons for change, the benefits it brings, and the risks of maintaining the status quo. By providing a compelling case for change, organizations can help individuals understand the necessity and importance of adopting new strategies.

Addressing Concerns: Acknowledging and addressing employees' concerns is essential for mitigating resistance. Leaders should create a safe space for open dialogue, actively listen to employees' worries, and address their questions and apprehensions. By empathizing with their concerns and providing thoughtful responses, organizations can alleviate fears and build trust.

Involving Employees: Involving employees in the planning and decision-making process helps them feel valued and heard. By seeking their input, organizations tap into their knowledge, experience, and creativity, which can lead to more effective and well-rounded strategies. Engaging employees in the strategic planning process fosters ownership and a sense of responsibility, making them more likely to embrace and support changes.

Change Management Strategies: Implementing change management strategies is crucial for guiding individuals through the transition process. This involves developing comprehensive plans that include education, training, and ongoing support. Education helps employees understand the new strategies and their implications, while training equips them with the necessary skills to adapt successfully. Ongoing support, such as coaching or mentoring, provides individuals with the assistance they need to navigate challenges and build confidence in new ways of working.

Leading by Example: Leaders play a crucial role in overcoming resistance to change. They should lead by example, demonstrating their commitment to the new strategies and embracing change themselves. When employees witness leaders actively participating in and supporting the change, it creates a positive influence and encourages others to follow suit.

Celebrating Successes: Recognizing and celebrating milestones and successes along the change journey helps reinforce the benefits of the new strategies and boosts morale. It creates a positive environment and motivates employees to continue embracing changes and actively contribute to their success.

Overcoming resistance to change requires patience, empathy, and a proactive approach. By employing effective communication, involving employees, providing support, and demonstrating strong leadership, organizations can foster a culture that embraces and adapts to new strategies. Ultimately, this enables successful strategy implementation and paves the way for organizational growth and innovation.

Lack of Accountability and Monitoring

Without proper monitoring and accountability mechanisms, strategic plans can become mere documents gathering dust on shelves. Organizations must establish clear metrics and key performance indicators (KPIs) to track progress, regularly review performance against objectives, and hold individuals and teams accountable for their responsibilities. By establishing a culture of accountability and continuous monitoring, organizations can ensure that strategies remain on track and are effectively executed.

Failure to Learn and Adapt

Organizations that do not learn from their experiences and adapt their strategies run the risk of becoming stagnant. Continuous learning and improvement are essential for long-term success. It is important to conduct post-implementation reviews, gather feedback, and encourage an environment where mistakes are seen as opportunities for growth. By embracing a learning mindset, organizations can iterate and refine their strategies, staying ahead of the curve.

In the realm of personal and organizational development, the concepts of single loop learning and double loop learning have gained significant attention. These two approaches to learning provide frameworks that encourage deeper reflection and the ability to adapt to complex challenges. Understanding the differences between single loop and double loop learning can empower individuals and organizations to enhance their problem-solving abilities and drive sustainable growth. Let's delve into these concepts and explore how they can revolutionize our learning processes.

Single Loop Learning

Single loop learning refers to the traditional approach of problem-solving and learning from experience. In this mode, individuals or organizations focus on fixing errors and improving their processes within existing frameworks. The emphasis is on identifying and rectifying specific actions or behaviors that led to undesired outcomes. It involves a linear cause-and-effect relationship, where adjustments are made to achieve desired results.

For instance, imagine a sales team that fails to meet their targets. In single loop learning, the team would analyze their sales techniques, identify areas for improvement, and implement changes to boost their performance. However, the underlying assumptions and strategies guiding their sales approach remain intact.

Double Loop Learning

Double loop learning, on the other hand, goes beyond merely fixing errors and addresses the underlying assumptions and mental models that shape our actions. It encourages individuals and organizations to question their fundamental beliefs, values, and decision-making processes. Double loop learning involves critical reflection on why certain actions were taken and whether they align with the desired outcomes.

Returning to the example of the sales team, in double loop learning, the team would question not only their sales techniques but also the broader strategies and assumptions that influenced their approach. They might ask themselves whether the targets were realistic, if the sales model itself needs to be reevaluated, or if there are external factors impacting their success.

Key Differences and Benefits

Depth of Reflection: Single loop learning focuses on fixing surface-level errors, while double loop learning prompts deeper reflection by challenging underlying assumptions and mental models.

Adaptability: Single loop learning is limited to incremental improvements, whereas double loop learning enables individuals and organizations to adapt to changing environments, identify new possibilities, and foster innovation.

Systemic Understanding: Double loop learning promotes a systemic understanding of problems, helping individuals and organizations grasp the bigger picture and make more informed decisions.

Transformational Change: Double loop learning has the potential to drive transformative change, leading to fundamental shifts in thinking, behavior, and strategies. It fosters a culture of continuous improvement and learning.

By recognizing and proactively addressing these challenges and pitfalls, organizations can enhance the effectiveness of their strategic planning efforts. A combination of open communication, thorough analysis, flexibility, strong execution, and a commitment to continuous learning will help organizations overcome obstacles and drive successful strategic outcomes. In the subsequent chapters, we will delve into developing a monitoring and developing strategy and best practices for addressing these challenges and ensuring the success of your strategic planning endeavors.

Chapter Seven: Monitoring and Evaluating Strategy

Monitoring and evaluating strategy is a critical component of successful strategic planning. It enables organizations to assess the progress of their strategic initiatives, measure performance against objectives, and make informed decisions to stay on track towards achieving their vision. This chapter explores the importance of monitoring and evaluating strategy and provides guidance on effective practices:

The Importance of Monitoring and Evaluation

Performance Measurement: monitoring and evaluation allow organizations to measure their performance against strategic objectives and key performance indicators (KPIs). It provides quantitative and qualitative data to assess progress and identify areas of improvement.

Adaptability and Agility: regular monitoring enables organizations to identify changes in the internal and external environment promptly. By staying informed about market trends, customer needs, and competitive dynamics, organizations can adjust their strategies and tactics accordingly.

Learning and Improvement: evaluation provides insights into what works and what does not. By analyzing successes and failures, organizations can learn from their experiences, refine their strategies, and continuously improve their performance.

Accountability and Transparency: monitoring and evaluation create a sense of accountability within the organization. It helps ensure that responsibilities are met, resources are utilized effectively, and progress is transparently communicated to stakeholders.

Key Elements of Effective Monitoring and Evaluation

Establishing Clear Objectives and KPIs: clear and measurable objectives are essential for effective monitoring and evaluation. Organizations should identify specific metrics and KPIs that align with their strategic objectives. These indicators should be realistic, measurable, and relevant to the organization's success.

Collecting and Analyzing Data: organizations need to collect relevant data to assess their performance. This includes both quantitative data (e.g., financial metrics, customer satisfaction ratings) and qualitative data (e.g., feedback from stakeholders, market research). Data analysis techniques, such as trend analysis, benchmarking, and comparison against industry standards, provide insights for decision-making.

Regular Reporting and Communication: timely reporting and communication ensure that stakeholders are informed about progress, achievements, and challenges. Regular updates and clear communication channels facilitate transparency and alignment throughout the organization.

Periodic Evaluation and Reviews: organizations should conduct periodic evaluations to assess the overall effectiveness of their strategies. These evaluations can take the form of post-implementation reviews, strategic reviews, or comprehensive audits. Evaluation findings provide valuable input for refining strategies and making informed decisions for future planning cycles.

Learning and Knowledge Sharing: monitoring and evaluation efforts should foster a culture of learning and knowledge sharing. Lessons learned from successes and failures should be documented and shared across the organization. This encourages continuous improvement and ensures that insights gained from monitoring and evaluation are applied to future planning cycles.

Effective Monitoring and Evaluation Practices

Establishing a Monitoring Framework: develop a framework that outlines the key elements of monitoring and evaluation, including objectives, indicators, data collection methods, and reporting mechanisms. This framework serves as a guide for consistent and systematic monitoring.

Utilizing Technology: leverage technology tools and software to streamline data collection, analysis, and reporting processes. Automation can enhance the accuracy, efficiency, and timeliness of monitoring and evaluation efforts.

Engaging Stakeholders: involve relevant stakeholders in the monitoring and evaluation process. This includes executives, managers, employees, customers, and other external partners. Their perspectives and feedback provide valuable insights and enhance the validity of evaluation findings.

Continuous Improvement: use evaluation findings to identify areas for improvement and refine strategies. Foster a culture that encourages experimentation, learning from failures, and iterative adaptation.

Adjusting Strategies: based on monitoring and evaluation results, make necessary adjustments to strategies, tactics, and resource allocation. This ensures that the organization remains responsive to changing internal and external factors.

By implementing effective monitoring and evaluation practices, organizations can track their progress, identify gaps, and make informed decisions to optimize their strategies. Monitoring and evaluation provide the necessary feedback loops to keep the organization focused, adaptable, and on the path to success. In the subsequent chapters, we will explore specific tools, techniques, and best practices for effective monitoring and evaluation of strategy.

Chapter Eight: Sustaining and Evolving Strategy

SUSTAINING AND EVOLVING strategy is vital for organizations to maintain their competitive edge and adapt to changing market dynamics. This chapter explores the importance of sustaining and evolving strategy and provides guidance on how organizations can achieve long-term success.

The Importance of Sustaining and Evolving Strategy

Adaptation to changing environment: business environments are dynamic and constantly evolving. Sustaining and evolving strategy enables organizations to respond to emerging opportunities, mitigate risks, and stay relevant in the face of changing market dynamics.

Competitive Advantage: continuous refinement and improvement of strategy allow organizations to create and maintain a competitive advantage. By identifying and leveraging unique capabilities, organizations can differentiate themselves from competitors and position themselves for long-term success.

Alignment with Vision and Mission: sustaining and evolving strategy ensures that the organization's actions and initiatives remain aligned with its vision and mission. It allows for course corrections and adjustments while staying true to the organization's overarching purpose and values.

Innovation and Growth: strategy evolution fosters an environment conducive to innovation and growth. By encouraging exploration of innovative ideas, embracing disruptive technologies, and fostering a culture of creativity, organizations can identify new avenues for growth and drive innovation within their industry.

Strategies for Sustaining and Evolving Strategy

Continuous environmental scanning: organizations must regularly monitor the internal and external environment to identify emerging trends, market shifts, and potential disruptors. This involves conducting market research, staying updated on industry developments, and analyzing customer feedback. The insights gained from environmental scanning inform strategy refinement and evolution.

Feedback and Learning Loops: create feedback mechanisms to gather insights from stakeholders, including customers, employees, and partners. This feedback can provide valuable information on areas for improvement and opportunities for innovation. Establishing learning loops within the organization allows for the dissemination of knowledge and the application of lessons learned to future strategic planning efforts.

Strategic Reviews and Assessments: conduct periodic strategic reviews to evaluate the effectiveness of the current strategy. Assess its alignment with the organization's vision, mission, and market conditions. Strategic reviews provide an opportunity to identify gaps, challenges, and areas where the strategy needs adjustment or innovation.

Innovation and Experimentation: foster a culture of innovation by encouraging experimentation and embracing calculated risks.

Allocate resources and create dedicated spaces for innovation, allowing employees to explore innovative ideas and test hypotheses. Embracing a fail-fast, learn-fast approach enables organizations to adapt quickly and make iterative improvements to their strategies.

Collaboration and Partnerships: forge strategic alliances and partnerships with external organizations that bring complementary expertise, resources, and capabilities. Collaborative efforts can help organizations expand their reach, access new markets, and co-create innovative solutions. Partnerships also facilitate knowledge sharing and provide fresh perspectives on strategy.

Leadership and Change Management: effective leadership is critical in sustaining and evolving strategy. Leaders must champion the need for change, communicate the vision, and guide the organization through the transition process. They should empower employees, foster a culture of agility and adaptability, and provide the necessary support and resources for strategy evolution.

Balancing Stability and Agility

Sustaining and evolving strategy requires striking a balance between stability and agility. While it is important to maintain consistency and stability in core strategic elements, organizations must also be open to adapt and pivot when necessary. This requires a flexible mindset, an appetite for innovation, and the ability to make informed decisions based on changing circumstances.

By adopting strategies for sustaining and evolving strategy, organizations can navigate the complexities of the business landscape, drive innovation, and achieve long-term success. Continual evaluation, adaptation, and alignment with the organization's vision and mission are key to thriving in a rapidly changing world.

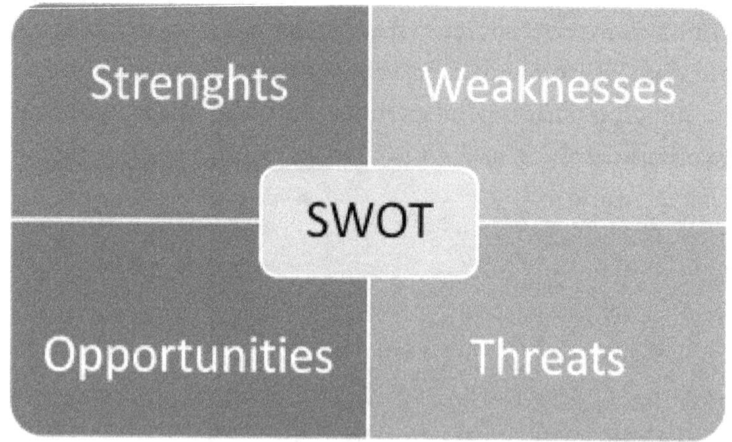

Chapter Nine: Conducting a SWOT Analysis

A SWOT analysis is a strategic planning tool used to evaluate the strengths, weaknesses, opportunities, and threats associated with a particular business or project. It provides a structured framework for assessing the internal and external factors that can impact an organization's success. Conducting a SWOT analysis helps organizations identify areas for improvement, capitalize on opportunities, and mitigate potential risks. The four steps to conduct a SWOT Analysis are to identify strengths, identify weaknesses, identify opportunities, and identify threats.

Identify Strengths (Internal)

Start by identifying the internal strengths of your organization. These are factors that give you a competitive advantage, such as unique capabilities, resources, expertise, or strong brand reputation. Consider aspects like your talented workforce, innovative products or services, efficient processes, strong financial position, or loyal customer base. Questions that should be asked are:

- What are our key competitive advantages?
- What unique resources, capabilities, or expertise do we possess?
- What aspects of our business consistently outperform competitors?
- What do customers value most about our products or services?
- What positive attributes distinguish us in the market?

Identify Weaknesses (Internal)

Next, evaluate the internal weaknesses or areas where your organization may be at a disadvantage compared to competitors. These can include factors such as outdated technology, limited resources, inadequate skills, poor customer service, or weak market presence. Be honest and critical in identifying areas that need improvement or pose challenges to your success. Questions that should be asked are:

- What areas of our business need improvement?
- What are our limitations or vulnerabilities?
- Where do we lag competitors?
- What negative feedback or complaints do we frequently receive?
- What internal challenges or obstacles hinder our performance?

Identify Opportunities (External)

Shift your focus to external factors that present opportunities for growth and success. These can include emerging market trends, changes in regulations, technological advancements, new customer segments, or untapped geographic markets. Identify potential areas where your organization can leverage its strengths to take advantage of these opportunities. Questions that should be asked are:

- What emerging market trends could benefit our business?
- Are there new customer segments or markets we can tap into?
- Are there technological advancements we can leverage?
- Are there changes in regulations or policies that create opportunities?
- Are there gaps or underserved areas in the market we can address?

Identify Threats (External)

Finally, consider external threats that could hinder your organization's performance or success. These can include factors such as intense competition, changing consumer preferences, economic downturns, disruptive technologies, or regulatory changes. Identify potential risks that could impact your organization's growth or sustainability. Questions that should be asked are:

- Who are our main competitors, and what are their

strengths?

- Are there new entrants in the market?
- Are there substitute products or services that could undermine our business?
- Are there changing customer preferences or behaviors that could impact us?
- Are there external factors such as economic, political, or environmental changes that pose risks?

Once you have identified the strengths, weaknesses, opportunities, and threats, you can analyze the findings and develop strategies that align with your organization's goals and objectives. Here is an example of conducting a SWOT analysis for a fictional company in the technology industry:

Strengths

- Highly skilled and experienced workforce.
- Strong brand reputation and recognition in the market.
- Cutting-edge technology and innovative product portfolio.
- Solid financial position with stable cash flow.
- Effective distribution network and strong partnerships with key suppliers.

Weaknesses

- Limited market presence in certain regions.
- Reliance on a single product line for a significant portion of revenue.

- Lack of diversification in customer base.
- High production costs lead to lower profit margins.
- Inefficiencies in internal processes and communication.

Opportunities

- Growing demand for technology products and services in emerging markets.
- Increasing adoption of cloud computing and digital transformation.
- Expansion into new customer segments, such as small and medium-sized enterprises (SMEs).
- Strategic partnerships with technology giants to leverage their distribution channels.
- Potential for mergers and acquisitions to gain market share and expand product offerings.

Threats

- Intense competition from established players in the market.
- Rapidly evolving technology landscape requiring continuous innovation.
- Economic volatility impacting customer spending patterns.
- Potential regulatory changes affecting the industry.
- Vulnerability to cybersecurity threats and data breaches.

Based on this SWOT analysis, the company can develop strategies to capitalize on its strengths, address weaknesses, seize opportunities, and mitigate threats. For example, they could focus on expanding into new geographic markets (leveraging strengths), diversifying their product portfolio (addressing weaknesses), investing in research and development to stay ahead of technological advancements (seizing opportunities), and enhancing cybersecurity measures to protect against threats.

Key Takeaway

It is important to note that a SWOT analysis should be regularly reviewed and updated as the business landscape evolves. It provides a snapshot of the current situation, but organizations should continually monitor and reassess their strengths, weaknesses, opportunities, and threats to stay agile and responsive to market dynamics.

Chapter Ten: Using Porter's Five Forces

Porter's Five Forces is a framework developed by Michael Porter, a renowned business strategist, to analyze the competitive dynamics and attractiveness of an industry. It helps organizations understand the competitive forces at play and make informed strategic decisions. The five forces include the threat of new entrants, the bargaining power of buyers, the bargaining power of suppliers, the threat of substitute products or services, and the intensity of competitive rivalry.

Identify the Threat of New Entrants

Assess the barriers to entry for new competitors in your industry. Consider factors such as economies of scale, brand loyalty, access to distribution channels, capital requirements, government regulations, and proprietary technology. High barriers make it difficult for new entrants to compete, resulting in a lower threat. Questions that should be asked are:

- What are the barriers to entry into our industry?
- Are there significant capital requirements for new entrants?
- Do economies of scale exist, giving established players a cost advantage?
- Are there regulatory or legal barriers that limit new entrants?
- How strong is brand loyalty or customer trust in existing competitors?

Assess the Bargaining Power of Buyers

Analyze the power and influence of your customers or buyers. Consider factors such as their volume of purchases, price sensitivity, switching costs, availability of substitutes, and the importance of your product or service to their business. If customers have strong bargaining power, they can demand lower prices or better terms, reducing your profitability. Questions that should be asked are:

- How price-sensitive are our customers?
- Do customers have many alternative options?
- Are there high switching costs for customers?
- How important is our product or service to our customers' business?
- Are there any purchasing volume or concentration factors that give buyers leverage?

Evaluate the Bargaining Power of Suppliers

Examine the power of your suppliers to influence your business. Factors to consider include the number of suppliers, uniqueness of their products or services, switching costs, availability of substitutes, and the importance of their inputs to your business. Suppliers with significant power can raise prices or limit supply, impacting your profitability. Questions that should be asked are:

- Do we rely on a small number of suppliers?
- Are there few alternatives for the inputs we require?
- Are there unique or specialized components or services that only a few suppliers can provide?

- Do suppliers have strong negotiating power due to their expertise or market dominance?
- Are there any supply chain risks that could disrupt our operations?

Assess the Threat of Substitute Products or Services

Identify potential substitutes that could fulfill the same customer needs. Consider factors such as price-performance trade-offs, ease of switching, and the availability of alternatives. The higher the availability and attractiveness of substitutes, the greater the threat they pose to your business. Questions that should be asked are:

- Are there alternative products or services that fulfill the same customer needs?
- How easy is it for customers to switch to substitute offerings?
- Are there price-performance trade-offs that make substitutes attractive?
- Are there emerging technologies or trends that could introduce new substitutes?
- How differentiated is our product or service compared to substitutes?

Analyze the Intensity of Competitive Rivalry

Evaluate the level of competition within your industry. Consider factors such as the number and size of competitors, industry growth rate, product differentiation, pricing strategies, and exit barriers. Highly competitive rivalry can result in price wars, reduced profitability, and the need for continuous innovation and differentiation. Questions that should be asked are:

- Who are our main competitors, and what are their strengths and weaknesses?
- How many competitors are there in our industry?
- Is the industry experiencing high growth or decline?
- Are there barriers to exit that keep competitors in the market?
- Are there frequent price wars, aggressive marketing, or constant product innovation?

Now, let's consider a detailed example of a Porter's Five Forces analysis for the smartphone industry:

Threat of New Entrants

- High capital requirements to establish manufacturing facilities and R&D capabilities act as barriers to entry.
- Established brands have strong brand loyalty and customer trust, making it difficult for new entrants to gain market share.
- Economies of scale in production and distribution provide competitive advantages to existing players.

Bargaining Power of Buyers

- Buyers have a wide range of choices and can easily switch between smartphone brands.
- Price sensitivity is high, and customers often compare features and prices before making a purchase.

- Increasing buyer knowledge and online platforms give them more bargaining power.

Bargaining Power of Suppliers

- Key suppliers of components, such as display panels and semiconductors, have strong bargaining power due to their specialized expertise and limited competition.
- The industry's high demand for certain components may lead to supply shortages and price fluctuations.
- Threat of Substitute Products or Services:
- The smartphone industry faces threats from substitute products such as tablets, laptops, and wearable devices that offer similar functionalities.
- Rapid technological advancements in other sectors may introduce new substitutes in the future.

Intensity of Competitive Rivalry

- The smartphone industry is highly competitive, with numerous global and local players vying for market share.
- Intense price competition and frequent product launches contribute to the rivalry.
- Established brands invest heavily in marketing, innovation, and distribution to maintain their market position.

Based on this analysis, organizations in the smartphone industry can develop strategies to address the competitive forces. For example, they can focus on building brand loyalty, leveraging economies of scale, negotiating favorable supplier contracts, investing in R&D for product differentiation, and adopting effective marketing and pricing strategies.

Key Takeaway

Porter's Five Forces analysis helps organizations gain a comprehensive understanding of their industry's competitive landscape. By identifying the forces at play, organizations can make informed decisions, develop strategies to capitalize on strengths and opportunities, and mitigate risks posed by external factors. It is important to conduct periodic reassessments to adapt to evolving industry dynamics.

Chapter Eleven: Using the Balanced Scorecard

THE BALANCED SCORECARD is a performance measurement and management framework that provides a balanced view of an organization's performance across multiple dimensions. It goes beyond financial metrics and incorporates strategic objectives, key performance indicators (KPIs), and targets related to various aspects of the business. The framework enables organizations to align their activities with their strategic goals and track progress in a comprehensive and balanced manner. The steps to effectively use The Balanced Scorecard are define strategic objectives, identify performance measures, set targets and initiatives, cascade to departments and individuals, and track and monitor progress.

Define Strategic Objectives

Identify the key strategic objectives that are critical for achieving your organization's mission and vision. These objectives should align with your overall strategy and reflect the areas of focus for your business. Examples may include improving customer satisfaction, increasing market share, enhancing operational efficiency, or fostering innovation.

Identify Performance Measures

Determine the specific metrics or KPIs that will be used to measure progress toward each strategic objective. Performance measures should be meaningful, quantifiable, and directly linked to the strategic objective they represent. For instance, customer satisfaction can be measured through metrics such as customer surveys, net promoter score (NPS), or customer retention rates.

Set Targets and Initiatives

Establish ambitious yet achievable targets for each performance measure. These targets should reflect the desired level of performance and support the organization's strategic goals. Additionally, identify specific initiatives or actions that will help drive progress and improve performance in each area.

Cascade to Departments and Individuals

Communicate the strategic objectives, performance measures, targets, and initiatives to relevant departments and individuals within the organization. Ensure that everyone understands their role in contributing to the overall objectives and how their performance will be measured and evaluated.

Track and Monitor Progress

Regularly collect data and track performance against the defined measures and targets. This can be done through ongoing monitoring, periodic reporting, and review sessions. Use the data to assess performance, identify trends, and take corrective actions when necessary.

Ask Key Questions

Throughout the process, ask relevant questions to evaluate the effectiveness of the Balanced Scorecard implementation:

- Are the chosen strategic objectives aligned with the

organization's mission and vision?

- Are the selected performance measures truly indicative of progress toward the objectives?
- Are the targets realistic and challenging enough to drive improvement?
- Are the initiatives and actions supporting the achievement of the objectives?
- Is the data collection process reliable and accurate?
- Are there any adjustments or refinements needed to improve the Balanced Scorecard implementation?

Here is a detailed example of a Balanced Scorecard for a fictional manufacturing company with four strategic objectives:

Objective 1

- Strategic Objective: Enhance Operational Efficiency
- Performance Measure: Overall Equipment Effectiveness (OEE)
- Target: Achieve OEE of 90% within the next year
- Initiatives: Implement preventive maintenance program, optimize production schedules, train employees on efficient equipment operation

Objective 2

- Strategic Objective: Improve Customer Satisfaction

- Performance Measure: Customer Satisfaction Index
- Target: Increase customer satisfaction score by 10% in the next six months

- Initiatives: Conduct customer feedback surveys, enhance customer service training, implement a customer complaint resolution process

Objective 3

- Strategic Objective: Foster Innovation
- Performance Measure: Number of New Product Development Projects
- Target: Launch three new products within the next year
- Initiatives: Establish a cross-functional innovation team, allocate dedicated resources for research and development, implement an idea management system

Objective 4

- Strategic Objective: Strengthen Employee Engagement
- Performance Measure: Employee Engagement Survey Results
- Target: Achieve an overall engagement score of 80% in the next survey
- Initiatives: Conduct regular employee feedback sessions, provide professional development opportunities, and implement recognition and reward programs

By using the Balanced Scorecard, the company can monitor progress and performance across these strategic objectives, ensuring a balanced focus on financial, customer, operational, and employee-related aspects. It enables the organization to make data-driven decisions, track alignment with strategic goals, and foster a culture of continuous improvement.

Chapter Twelve: Using Strategy Mapping

STRATEGY MAPPING IS a visual representation of an organization's strategy that helps align activities and initiatives with strategic objectives. It provides a clear and comprehensive view of how different components of the business are interconnected and contribute to the achievement of strategic goals. Strategy mapping enables organizations to communicate and cascade their strategy effectively, understand cause-and-effect relationships, and identify areas of focus for performance improvement. Here are the steps to utilize this strategy tool.

Define Strategic Objectives

Identify the key strategic objectives that reflect your organization's mission and long-term goals. These objectives should be specific, measurable, actionable, realistic, and time-bound (SMART).

Determine Cause-and-Effect Relationships

Identify the cause-and-effect relationships between different strategic objectives. Understand how achieving one objective influences the success of others. This step helps create a logical flow of how strategic objectives are interconnected.

Select Key Performance Indicators (KPIs)

Determine the appropriate KPIs that will measure progress toward each strategic objective. KPIs should be aligned with the objectives they represent and provide meaningful insights into performance.

Map the Strategy

Create a visual representation of the strategy map, usually in the form of a diagram. Start with the top-level strategic objectives and then link them to the lower-level objectives. Use arrows or lines to indicate the cause-and-effect relationships between the objectives.

Identify Strategic Initiatives

Determine the initiatives, projects, or actions that will contribute to the achievement of each strategic objective. These initiatives should address the underlying factors that drive success in each objective.

Cascade to Departments and Individuals

Communicate the strategy map to relevant departments and individuals within the organization. Ensure that everyone understands how their activities and initiatives align with the strategic objectives.

Monitor and Review

Continuously monitor and review the progress of the strategy implementation. Regularly assess the performance of the KPIs and adjust initiatives as needed to ensure alignment with the strategic objectives.

During the process of strategy mapping, it is crucial to ask relevant questions to ensure the effectiveness of the approach. Some key questions to consider include:

- Are the chosen strategic objectives aligned with the organization's mission and vision?
- Have we identified all the cause-and-effect relationships between the objectives?
- Are the selected KPIs meaningful and directly linked to the objectives they represent?
- Are strategic initiatives and actions addressing the underlying factors that drive success?
- Is the strategy map effectively communicated and understood by all stakeholders?
- Are there any adjustments or refinements needed to improve the strategy map and its implementation?

Here is a detailed example of a strategy map for a fictional healthcare organization:

Objective 1

Strategic Objective: Improve Patient Experience

- Lower-Level Objective: Reduce Patient Waiting Time
    - KPI: Average Waiting Time
    - Initiatives: Streamline patient registration process, optimize appointment scheduling, implement digital check-in systems.
- Lower-Level Objective: Enhance Communication with Patients

- ○ KPI: Patient Satisfaction with Communication
- ○ Initiatives: Implement patient portals for secure communication, provide regular updates on test results and treatment plans, enhance staff training on effective communication.

Objective 2

Strategic Objective: Achieve Operational Excellence

- Lower-Level Objective: Improve Process Efficiency
  - ○ KPI: Process Cycle Time
  - ○ Initiatives: Implement Lean Six Sigma methodologies, conduct process mapping and analysis, automate manual processes where possible.
- Lower-Level Objective: Optimize Resource Utilization
  - ○ KPI: Resource Utilization Rate
  - ○ Initiatives: Conduct resource allocation analysis, implement capacity planning tools, improve inventory management practices.

By using a strategy map, the organization can clearly see how improving patient experience and achieving operational excellence are interconnected. It helps align initiatives and resources to the strategic objectives, enabling a focused and coordinated approach to strategy implementation. Regular monitoring of the KPIs allows the organization to track progress and make informed decisions for continuous improvement.

Chapter Thirteen: Conducting a PESTEL Analysis

PESTEL analysis is a framework used to assess the external factors that impact an organization's business environment. It examines the political, economic, social, technological, environmental, and legal factors that can influence the organization's operations, strategies, and decision-making.

Political

Consider the political stability, government policies, regulations, trade agreements, and political trends that may affect the organization.

Economic

Assess the overall economic conditions, such as GDP growth, inflation rates, interest rates, exchange rates, and consumer spending patterns.

Social

Analyze the demographic factors, cultural norms, social attitudes, lifestyle trends, and consumer behavior that could impact the organization.

Technological

Evaluate the technological advancements, innovation trends, automation, digitalization, and infrastructure that may affect the industry or organization.

Environmental

Consider the environmental concerns, sustainability practices, climate change, natural disasters, and ecological factors that impact the organization.

Legal

Examine the legal and regulatory frameworks, industry-specific regulations, intellectual property laws, labor laws, and compliance requirements.

Research and Gather Data:

Conduct thorough research and gather relevant data for each factor. Utilize a variety of sources such as industry reports, government publications, market research, and expert opinions to obtain accurate and up-to-date information.

Analyze and Assess:

Identify the potential opportunities or advantages that arise from each factor.

Determine the potential risks, challenges, or threats posed by each factor.

Assess the level of impact and significance of each factor on the organization.

Ask Key Questions: To extract valuable insights from the analysis, ask pertinent questions related to each factor:

- How might political changes or government policies

impact the organization's operations or market access?
- What economic trends or factors could influence consumer purchasing power or demand for the organization's products or services?
- What social shifts or cultural changes could impact customer preferences or market trends?
- What technological advancements or disruptions could impact the organization's industry or business model?
- What environmental factors or sustainability practices could affect the organization's operations or reputation?
- What legal and regulatory requirements or changes could impact the organization's compliance or operations?

Evaluate Findings: Synthesize the findings from the analysis to understand the overall implications for the organization. Identify the key trends, opportunities, and challenges that emerge from the PESTEL analysis.

Here is a detailed example of a PESTEL analysis for a fictional technology company entering a new international market:

Political: Analyze the political stability of the target country, government regulations on technology imports, policies on intellectual property protection, and trade agreements affecting industry.

Economic: Evaluate the country's economic growth rate, currency exchange rates, inflation levels, consumer purchasing power, and economic indicators specific to the technology sector.

Social: Consider the target market's demographic trends, cultural preferences, social attitudes toward technology, and consumer behavior related to technology adoption.

Technological: Assess the local technological infrastructure, level of digitalization, availability of skilled tech workforce, and technological advancements specific to the industry.

Environmental: Evaluate the country's environmental regulations, sustainability practices, consumer awareness of environmental issues, and any potential impact of the organization's technology on the environment.

Legal: Examine the local legal framework for technology companies, intellectual property laws, data protection regulations, and compliance requirements.

Through the PESTEL analysis, the technology company can gain insights into the external factors that may influence its market entry strategy, product customization, pricing, regulatory compliance, and marketing approach in the new international market. It helps the organization identify opportunities, mitigate risks, and make informed decisions to navigate the external business environment effectively.

CHAPTER FOURTEEN: USING Hoshin Kanri

Hoshin Kanri, also known as Policy Deployment, is a strategic planning and management methodology that originated in Japan. It aims to align organizational goals and objectives with individual actions and measures. Hoshin Kanri provides a structured approach for cascading strategic initiatives throughout an organization and ensures a systematic and focused approach to achieving long-term objectives. The steps for utilizing Hoshin Kanri are establishing the strategic vision, identifying key objectives, developing annual objectives, cascading objectives, developing action plans, deploying measures and metrics, and review and adjust.

Establish the Strategic Vision

Clearly define the organization's long-term vision, mission, and strategic objectives. This provides the foundation for the Hoshin Kanri process and ensures alignment across all levels of the organization.

Identify Key Objectives

Identify the critical objectives that will drive the organization's strategic success. These objectives should be specific, measurable, achievable, relevant, and time-bound (SMART). Each objective should contribute to the overall vision and mission.

Develop Annual Objectives

Break down the long-term objectives into actionable annual objectives. These annual objectives should be challenging yet attainable within the given timeframe. They should align with the long-term objectives and provide a clear direction for the organization.

Cascade Objectives

Cascade the objectives throughout the organization, ensuring alignment from top management to frontline employees. Each level of the organization should have its own set of objectives that contribute to the achievement of the higher-level objectives.

Develop Action Plans

Develop detailed action plans to achieve the objectives at each level. These plans outline the specific initiatives, projects, tasks, and milestones required to accomplish the objectives. Assign responsibilities and timelines to ensure accountability and progress tracking.

Deploy Measures and Metrics

Define the key performance indicators (KPIs) and metrics that will be used to measure progress toward each objective. Establish targets and develop a system for tracking and monitoring the performance of these measures.

Review and Adjust

Conduct regular reviews and assessments of progress. Monitor the performance against the objectives and KPIs and identify areas that require adjustments or improvement. Make necessary changes to the action plans and measures to stay on track and address emerging challenges.

When conducting Hoshin Kanri, it is essential to ask relevant questions to ensure its effectiveness. Here are some key questions to consider:

- Are the objectives aligned with the organization's long-term vision and mission?
- Are the objectives challenging yet achievable within the given timeframe?
- Is there a clear cascading of objectives throughout the organization?
- Are the action plans well-defined, with assigned responsibilities and timelines?
- Are the chosen measures and metrics aligned with the objectives and reflective of success?
- Are there any obstacles or risks that may hinder the achievement of the objectives?
- Are the resources, capabilities, and support systems in place to execute the action plans effectively?

Here is an example of Hoshin Kanri in a manufacturing company:

Strategic Objective: Improve Overall Equipment Efficiency (OEE)

Annual Objective 1: Reduce Equipment Downtime by 20%

- Action Plan: Implement preventive maintenance program, conduct equipment audits, provide training for maintenance personnel, and establish a real-time monitoring system.

- Measures: Equipment Downtime, Mean Time Between Failures (MTBF), Mean Time to Repair (MTTR).

Annual Objective 2: Increase Production Line Efficiency by 15%

- Action Plan: Implement Lean manufacturing principles, conduct value stream mapping, train operators on standardized work procedures, and optimize production schedules.
- Measures: Production Line Efficiency, Cycle Time, Scrap Rate.

Annual Objective 3: Improve Employee Engagement and Skills

- Action Plan: Implement regular feedback sessions, provide skill development training, establish recognition and reward programs, and promote a culture of continuous improvement.
- Measures: Employee Engagement Survey Results, Training Hours per Employee, Employee Turnover Rate.

Through Hoshin Kanri, the company aligns its strategic objective of improving OEE with specific annual objectives that are cascaded down to different levels of the organization. Action plans, measures, and metrics are developed to track progress and ensure accountability. Regular reviews and adjustments are made to address any obstacles or changes in the business environment.

Hoshin Kanri helps the organization focus on strategic priorities, improve communication and alignment, and drive continuous improvement throughout the organization. It enables the effective execution of strategic objectives and enhances overall performance and competitiveness.

Conclusion

In the dynamic and competitive business landscape, strategic planning is a vital process for organizations to achieve their goals, drive success, and sustain long-term growth. "Your Strategy, Your Success" has explored various aspects of strategic planning, providing insights and guidance to help organizations develop effective strategies.

Throughout the book, we have covered essential components of successful strategy, including a clear and compelling vision, thorough analysis and understanding, alignment with mission and values, differentiation and competitive advantage, flexibility and adaptability, implementation and execution, and continuous monitoring and evaluation. By incorporating these components into their strategic planning efforts, organizations can enhance their ability to navigate challenges, capitalize on opportunities, and achieve their desired outcomes.

We also delved into overcoming common challenges and pitfalls in the strategic planning process. By addressing issues such as lack of clarity and alignment, insufficient analysis and understanding, resistance to change, and inadequate implementation and execution, organizations can overcome obstacles and increase the effectiveness of their strategic planning endeavors.

Furthermore, we explored the significance of monitoring and evaluating strategy. By establishing clear objectives and key performance indicators, collecting and analyzing relevant data, and engaging stakeholders in the monitoring process, organizations can assess their progress, make data-driven decisions, and ensure alignment with their strategic objectives. Regular evaluation and continuous improvement enable organizations to adapt their strategies and remain agile in an ever-changing business environment.

Sustaining and evolving strategy emerged as another crucial aspect of strategic planning. By continuously monitoring the internal and external environment, gathering feedback, conducting strategic reviews, fostering innovation, and embracing partnerships, organizations can sustain their competitive advantage and evolve their strategies to meet changing market dynamics and customer needs.

As we conclude this book, it is important to emphasize that strategic planning is not a one-time event but an ongoing process. It requires commitment, collaboration, and a willingness to learn and adapt. By applying the principles and strategies discussed in this book, organizations can navigate the complexities of the business landscape and position themselves for long-term success.

Remember, your strategy is the blueprint for your organization's success. It provides direction, aligns efforts, and empowers you to make informed decisions. Embrace strategic planning as a continuous journey, and let "your strategy, your success" be your guide as you navigate the ever-evolving business landscape and unlock your organization's full potential.

About the Author

William Chesnutt was born and raised in South Texas until he joined the United States Marine Corps in July 2001. Little did he know that a couple of months later, the country would be at war. He attended Air Traffic Control School in Pensacola, Florida and became a certified Federal Aviation Administration Air Traffic Controller. His career in the Marine Corps spanned a little more than 20 years and included three tours to Iraq and one year deployment to Afghanistan. He also lived and visited the Philippines, South Korea, Japan, Thailand, and Okinawa. He spent three years at the Staff Noncommissioned Officer Academy on Marine Corps Base Camp Pendleton as a Faculty Advisor where he taught more than 2,000 students in the areas of Personnel Administration, Planning, Training, Leadership, and Culture. He retired from the Marine Corps in July 2021.

William worked as an independent consultant for two years (2019-2021) implementing continuous improvement and quality management programs for organizations in Southern California and trained more than three hundred students at the Lean Six Sigma Yellow and Green Belt levels. At the same time, he volunteered as a small business mentor for SCORE, a national nonprofit that provides free business coaching and mentoring, where he mentored more than 40 businesses across the country and co-launched a five-day virtual workshop for veterans that allowed them to take their business ideas from just an idea to business started in five weeks. He continues his nonprofit work to this day as a Board Member for The Defeating Epilepsy Foundation. He has continued his business mentoring work with Newchip Accelerator where he mentors businesses in the areas of business planning, financial modeling and forecasting, industry research, go-to market strategy, acquiring pre-seed, seed, and series funding, building the right team and organizational culture, development of minimum viable products, and development of pitch decks.

William's educational achievements include a Bachelor of Science in Information Technology Management, a Master of Arts in Management with a concentration in Organizational Leadership, a Graduate Certificate in Human Capital Leadership, and a Graduate Certificate in Logistics Management from American Military University. He also obtained a Master of Business Administration from the University of Redlands, a Certificate in Design Thinking from the University of California Riverside, and a Certificate in Business Law from California State University Long Beach. He is a certified Lean Six Sigma Master Black Belt and a Resilience-Building Leadership Professional – Trainer. He is currently pursuing his Doctor of Business Administration with a concentration in Organizational Leadership and Development from Capella University.

William is the Founder and Chief Executive Officer for the Strategic Development Group LLC, a management consulting and training company and Strategic U, an online learning academy. He is also an Adjunct Faculty member for the School of Business at University of the People.

In William's free time, he enjoys going to Major League Baseball games, hiking, taking road trips, and spending time with his family.